CONVERSATIONS WITH MOM
Life Lessons of Love, Leadership, and Legacy

JURLINE K. REDEAUX, MSW

CONVERSATIONS WITH MOM
Life Lessons of Love, Leadership, and Legacy

JURLINE K. REDEAUX, MSW
Conversations with Mom:

Life Lessons of Love, Leadership, and Legacy
Copyright © 2021 by Jurline Redeaux
Published by Jurline Redeaux
Book Cover Design Sophisticated Press LLC

PRINTED IN THE UNITED STATES OF AMERICA ISBN
978-0-578-83713-0

Scripture quotations from
The Authorized (King James) Version.

Rights in the Authorized Version in the United Kingdom are vested in the Crown. Reproduced by permission of the Crown's patentee, Cambridge University Press

ACKNOWLEDGEMENTS

This book is dedicated to my Mother Ola Mae Sutton Johnson. Against all odds she chose to give me life. I'm thankful to God for blessing me with a God-fearing Mother. I would be remiss if I did not thank the Village that supported us: my Grandmother Ethel Hemings Ivy the Harriet Tubman of our family, my great Aunt Johnie Jefferson the historian, and my Aunt Ruth Ivy Joyner my Sheroe, who encouraged me to "go big or stay home." To my big brother John Johnson, my last surviving sibling— we share an unbreakable bond that has lasted for over sixty-nine years. Your early investment in my life paid off and I thank you. To my sister, friend, mentor, coach, and counselor, Juana Harper. Thank you for believing in me long before I believed in myself.

To all my extended family, mentors, and mentee's, thanks for believing in me.

There is no way I could have written this book without the support of my daughter Levonnia Patrice Redeaux Iwouha. You are my best friend, colleague, and prayer partner. Finally, I give thanks to my grandchildren: Nelson, Naomi, and Noah Iwouha. For your unconditional love this one is for you!

TABLE OF CONTENTS

Introduction - Love the Beginning 1

Chapter 1 - The Delta To USC 5

Chapter 2 - The Great Migration 9

Chapter 3 - Leadership 13

Chapter 4 - Mother Knows Best (Mother Wit) 17

Prologue - Transitions 25

INTRODUCTION

LOVE THE BEGINNING

A Mother's love is unconditional. Dear Mama, when I read 1 Corinthians 13:3-7, I'm reminded of how you loved the world and everyone in the world, especially me.

Mama, we spent forty-three wonderful years together. I am filled with such a deep sense of pride, love, and yet some sadness. You shared your heart with so many, your love changed countless lives, but most importantly created mine.

THE GREATEST GIFT

I CORINTHIANS 13 NKJV

¹³ Though I speak with the tongues of men and of angels, but have not love, I have become sounding brass or a clanging cymbal. ² And though I have *the gift of* prophecy, and understand all mysteries and all knowledge, and though I have all faith, so that I could remove mountains, but have not love, I am nothing. ³ And though I bestow all my goods to feed *the poor,* and though I give my body to be burned, but have not love, it profits me nothing.

⁴ Love suffers long *and* is kind; love does not envy; love does not parade itself, is not puffed up; ⁵ does not behave rudely, does not seek its own, is not provoked, thinks no evil; ⁶ does not rejoice in iniquity, but rejoices in the truth; ⁷ bears all things, believes all things, hopes all things, endures all things.

⁸ Love never fails. But whether *there are* prophecies, they will fail; whether *there are* tongues, they will cease; whether *there is* knowledge, it will vanish away. ⁹ For we know in part and we prophesy in part. ¹⁰ But when that which is perfect has come, then that which is in part will be done away.

¹¹ When I was a child, I spoke as a child, I understood as a child, I thought as a child; but when I became a man, I put away childish things. ¹² For

now we see in a mirror, dimly, but then face to face. Now I know in part, but then I shall know just as I also am known.

[13] And now abide faith, hope, love, these three; but the greatest of these *is* love.

CHAPTER 1

THE DELTA TO USC

The Mississippi Delta, in the year of my birth, must have been a difficult time for African American people. I can still hear and feel the sorrow in your voice when you would reminisce about your days of extreme poverty, hunger, and unbearable heat in the Summer and cold in the Winters. However, you never complained. You were living proof of 1 Corinthians 13: 3-7.

Since your passing in 1994, I have read a great deal about the Mississippi Delta. The year you passed away I was in graduate school, at the University Of Southern California (USC) studying to become a Social Worker. Unfortunately, I never got to tell you that you were the inspiration behind my decision. Because of you, I became a Social Worker.

In your later years, I watched you struggle with so many emotional hurdles. Hurdles that would have sent the average person to the crazy house. In your case, Mama, it was your Faith in God that kept you resilient and sane. In 1949, you were deserted , in Clarksdale, Mississippi by your husband Willie Johnson. Though there was much secrecy behind my birth, I was the youngest and the only girl of four boys. Come to think of it, we had far too many commonalities that we never discussed. For instance, in 1984, my then husband, your favorite son in law, Frederick

Redeaux III whom you lovingly referred to as "Fred" also deserted me with two children in Cherry Point, North Carolina, with no means to survive.

Regardless of it all, Mama, you were such an amazing role model. Though you never fully disclosed the details behind my birth, you raised me with confidence. I will never undermine the courage it took for you to give birth to me. Stranded and alone you were left with four small boys to house, feed, and clothe, all with no money. Yet you still gave me a chance. You were truly a 1 Corinthians 13 Woman.

Thankfully, you, my birth certificate, and my great aunt finally gave me some insight on my conception. I remember my sigh of relief when I found out Willie Johnson was not my Father. As the story goes, you met my birth Father, who remains unnamed, although his name is on my birth certificate. (Midwives kept it real!) And the love between you both blossomed into little old me. My Great Aunt told me all about him. She said he was a good man, hardworking, and even father like to your four boys. To the extent that he would even cut their hair. I can only imagine how relieved and cared for you must have felt.

Mama, I wished we could have spoken more about "my Daddy." My brother, Sonny, tells me "my Daddy" was the hand that helped us back up. "my Daddy" truly loved us and cared for us. Though I remember very little of "my Daddy" I vaguely remember meeting him. Once, in my nine year old eyes, he appeared to be a good person, tall, tan, and slender. Most definitely good looking! I know for sure I inherited some good genes from "my Daddy" who was compassionate and courageous.

As I look back on what your life may have looked like, I know it must have been hard. Pregnant, with a child out of wedlock, it took a great deal of fortitude to preserve. Life was not easy for you. But I do wish to thank you Mama, for giving me life. You didn't have to do it. Your early life struggles is what kept me going went things is my life appeared upside down You never complained. You were truly one of a kind.

As I mentioned earlier, our life had so many parallels. I too met a Marine after Fred left us. I fell in love with him because he loved my kids. Mama, I know how it feels to be deserted by your husband, and how it feels to fall for someone who loves your kids. In spite of all precautions, I became pregnant. However, my lover already had two kids and did not want anymore. Therefore, I did not have the courage to go at it alone so I chose to have an abortion. It was a sad time for the both of us, however, I could not bring a life into the world with no Father. Mama, you truly embody what it means to love beyond measure. I thank you for giving me life.

CHAPTER 2

THE GREAT MIGRATION

The Great Migration was the mass movement of about five million southern blacks to the North and West between 1915 and 1960. During the initial wave the majority of migrants moved to major northern cities such as Chicago, Illinois, Detroit, Michigan, Pittsburgh, Pennsylvania, and New York, New York. By World War II the migrants continued to move North but many of them headed west to Los Angeles, Oakland, San Francisco, California, Portland, Oregon, and Seattle, Washington.[1]

Our family was among the many families that moved to Chicago seeking better financial opportunities. Prior to moving, my parents were sharecroppers. The conditions were dismal, long hours, and little pay. I remember the stories of how Grandmama had to nurse both you and her sister, Aunt Johnie Mae because their Mother had passed away. According to family, in the fields there was no time off. Yet, the part that resonated with me most was when you spoke of going to school. Your voice was filled with excitement and joy as you told the tales of attending the one room schoolhouse. Then suddenly, your voice would become remorseful when you spoke of only making it to third grade because you had to quit school to work in the cotton fields. Your sorrow made me more determined to finish my education at all cost.

Though I was the only member of the family that escaped working in the fields, I also was the last one to migrate to Chicago. As the story goes, you returned to Willie Johnson, your husband, along with my four older brothers. I stayed behind with Grandmother, and she and I traveled to Chicago when I was three months old. . Grandmama knew how difficult it would be for you to So Grandmama handled it. This secure foundation prepared me for the day that I reunited with the family.. Mama, this is why I must tell the world about our amazing bond, the difficulty of your early life, subsequent marriage, separation, and then an out of wedlock birth. My hope is my telling our story, others will recognize that it does not matter where one starts, it matters how one finishes the race called

---

[1] Christensen, "The Great Migration", 1.

life. As a parent, I was able to draw strength from the courage it took for you to raise me against all odds.

My migration continued as I transitioned from living with Grandmama to living with "our family." It was difficult but I eventually found my place. Your love gave me all the confidence I needed, I was your daughter and we were all a good fit.

The economic conditions were not any better in Chicago. I remember our first apartment. It was a cold-water flat with a shared bathroom. It was on Oakwood, the Southside of Chicago. Mama, if only you could see it now, it is all gentrified as the Caucasians discovered the "Vintage Apartments" and refurbished them. The best part about that cold-water flat was when my sister Patricia was born. I have vague memories of her, but I remember the smell of baby oil and that castile baby soap. It was comforting to think of my little sister. Daddy finally had his little girl.

Unfortunately, tragedy was lurking and that tragedy has made me into the activist that I am today. Chicago was just as segregated then as it is now. We were subjected to the same Jim Crow Laws that were in the South, just packaged differently. Although I only know bits and pieces of the story; I never forget the pain. Patricia became ill at only sixteen months and when you took her to the nearest hospital, Mt. Sinai, which was all White at the time, you were told that there was nothing wrong and to go back home. However, she didn't get better, so you and Daddy drove her from the Southside to the West Side of Chicago, where the Cook County Hospital was located. At that time, The Dyan Ryan Freeway had not been built, so it must have been a long agonizing drive with a very sick baby. As it turns out, Patricia had pneumonia and she died in your arms.

Mama, I am sad as I type this, I vaguely remember the funeral, but I do recollect the sadness hanging over the family. Everybody loved her,

Daddy called her "Tweet." By all accounts, her death totally devastated him. I can't imagine how you coped with this significant loss. Though it was never spoken of, I can only imagine the impact it had on your marriage.

Mama, only God could have pulled you through. You never knew, but I often wondered if Daddy wished it would have been me. Yet, I hid this within me. I was determined to make you both proud. I would seek Justice for our precious Patricia through my work. I made a decision to fight for equal treatment for all. I became an advocate/activist from that point on. Patricia's story shaped the course of my life. Her legacy lives on in your grandchildren. Your son Larry named his daughter Kimberly Patrice Johnson. I named my daughter, Levonnia Patrice Redeaux. Your baby Patricia will never be forgotten.

As time made way, we rebounded. The family moved to the Henry Horner Projects on the Westside, and finally we purchased our home with Daddy's VA Benefits. You preserved through it all. Our family endured all things, but love still persevered.

CHAPTER 3

LEADERSHIP

Mama, you were a Servant Leader. Leading while serving others, that is how I viewed you.. You gave without expecting anything in return, that's how selfless you were. When we lived in the Henry Horner Projects, your leadership skills were remarkable. Everyone came to you. Whether they needed a cup of sugar, a cup of flour, a listening ear, a babysitter, or most importantly shelter. You never turned anyone away. Through you I learned compassion and empathy.

You were a leader in our Community. *Miss Johnson* was your official name. You counseled so many young mothers. On several occasions, you even provided refuge to a woman escaping her abusive husband. That woman knew Miss *Johnson* would provide support. I learned many things from you Mama, but one of the most important leadership skills I learned was not to gossip. I never heard you discuss anyone's situation. People knew that they could trust you with their secrets.

Mama, you raised countless generations of children, including my own. You treated each of them as your own. Through your nurturance , most of the youth that spent summers in your backyard went on to become leaders in the community and ultimately became servant leaders. They are in all helping professions: Nursing, Police Officers, Navy Chief, and Supervising Social Workers. Your legacy of leadership is one that keeps on giving. I am so proud to be your daughter.

My two children, Frederick and Levonnia spent every Summer with you. You helped raise them along with so many others. Your grandson Frederick, retired as a Navy Chief. Your granddaughter, Levonnia who you affectionately called (Vonnie), followed in my footsteps. She is now a Supervising Social Worker at DCFS and also obtained her Master's Degree in Social Work from the University of Southern California, twenty years after I obtained mine. She accomplished this while raising three children and working all at the same time.

Whilst being *Miss Johnson*, you never stopped being our Mama. You participated in the Parents Teachers Association (PTA). You never missed a meeting and was always the first to volunteer when needed. You were extraordinary.

Finally, your Leadership was evident in the Church. You taught me the importance of working in the Church. You didn't believe in being a "bench warmer." You played an active role in every Church you joined. During the last season of your life you continued to serve. I was so proud when you were selected to join the *Mother Board* at your final home church, *Israel Tabernacle*.

You always looked so regal in your white dress and rarely missed a Sunday. Once again, whenever there was a need, they called on *Mother Johnson*. One of my fondest memories was seeing both Frederick and Levonnia on the Altar with Reverend Morris. Frederick an Altar boy and was seated next to Reverend Morris. On the other hand, Levonnia was seated on his lap, because he refused to allow us to chastise her when she was acting out. He gave us that stern look, and said, "bring that baby to me." I never told you how proud I was to see both of them on the Altar.

The seeds of your Leadership run deep. I remember in Graduate school telling one of my Professors that you were the first Social Worker in our family. She was surprised and asked what your name was, thinking you were one of them. I proudly said, "My Mother was the first Social Worker in my life." She of course was shocked when I went on to tell her that I learned leadership, compassion, and ethics from you. That was a fun day!

CHAPTER 4

MOTHER KNOWS BEST (MOTHER WIT)

Mama, your legacy is one that has been passed down from one generation to the next. I know most of you have heard the saying, "Mother knows best." It has always been a tradition that mothers seem to know everything when it comes to life, love, and punishment. Yes, I said, punishment. I am not talking about corporal punishment, although I endured a few spankings from my Mother, usually with a switch. I am talking about the punishments that come from not living by God's law. Yes, one of the best legacies Mama taught me was to be God fearing.

The reason I call this the fun chapter, is because it consists of "Mama sayings." I bet as you have gotten older, you hear yourself repeating them as well.

Mama always had sayings. Mama sayings, sometimes called *Mother Wit*, have served me better than any one of my college degrees. I hope you too find them helpful and refreshing. Below are a few that I still use to this very day. Those that know me well, are familiar with most of them, because I am always saying, "What did you say Mama?" Then I would answer with one of her sayings:

1. Nothing beats a failure by a try.

This one is so profound when you think about it. Mama in this one was saying, go for whatever you wish to achieve, if it works great, not giving it a try is an automatic failure!

2. What goes around comes around.

We smart types, call this Karma. However, what Mama meant was, if you do something wrong or vice versa, it will catch up to you. For this reason, oftentimes when someone did me wrong, I wanted to get back at them. However, I remember this saying, and take comfort, it is going to catch up with them.

3. What is done in the dark will come to light.

Now this one kept me from getting in trouble. It seems Mama had a secret way of figuring out what you had been up to. Now as an adult, I realize it and most of you do too. I give one example, Politicians. Their dirt usually is exposed sooner or later. In other words, don't think that cheating or sneaking around won't be exposed. Believe me, this one is true.

4. Don't let the right hand know what the left hand is doing.

Keep your mouth shut! Don't tell everyone your business. I am still learning this one. When I was growing up, Mama would use this saying in context which helped me to understand how shrewd she was in how she dealt with her business.

5. All that Glitters Ain't Gold.

One of my favorites. I used to covet others' success and the women that had the fine men. Then I would remember Mama saying, "Honey just because that man might look good, just remember all the glitters ain't gold." You better believe it, this one served me well. Just because it looks good don't mean it is good for you.

6. Even Iron Wears Out.

Mama was well before her time, she taught me about self-care before it became a buzzword. When Mama used this one, it would be when she felt pressured or overwhelmed. She would say, "Jurl,(my nickname) even Iron wears out!" Lord, My Mama was a genius. This saying taught me the importance of knowing how to say, enough is enough.

7. If God be for you, it is more than the World against you.

Once again, Mama's wisdom and her faith. I grew up knowing that no matter what, if I had God in my life, no matter what life challenges came my way, I would make it through! Can I get a witness?

8. What is meant for you, you will get it.

This saying has sustained me, when I was truly discouraged. It seems that the things I prayed for and wanted so badly simply eluded me. When I was finished crying and feeling sorry for myself, this saying would comfort me.

9. Two wrongs don't make it right.

This is still the foundation of my core existence. This is hard to embrace, when you want to get even with someone for wronging you. Once again,

My Mama's wisdom sustains me. During my lifetime, I have been falsely accused and misunderstood so many times. In the end, I did what was right. It is easier to get even. Where does that leave you?

10. God don't let nothing slip up on you.

This one right here. I have to say has had the most impact as I have gotten older and developed a closer walk with God. Once again, Mama would say this one when God revealed a premonition of something that was going to happen. When it happened, she would simply say, "I am not surprised because God don't let nothing slip up on you." I now am able to attest to that as it has empowered me to know that God given wisdom will sustain you.

11. God Makes a Way out of No way.

This saying shows my Mother's deep abiding faith. In spite of all the hardships she faced, she held onto this belief. I have seen it manifest in my own life. During my lifetime, I have been on the brink of losing everything, even my sanity. But God! He made a way.

12. There is always a Ram in the Bush.

To be honest, when I was growing up, I had no idea who the Ram was and where the bush was located. However, the way she used it in context allowed me to figure out that in spite of all odds, God would provide. Later when I began to study the Bible, I was able to put the two together. What an amazing Woman of Faith!

13. You will reap what you sow.

I am sure many of you heard this one. Growing up, this saying had a tremendous impact on the way I treated others and conducted my life. Sow good and you reap good. Sow bad and you reap bad. It was inherent in my being that whatever seeds you sow, kindness or goodness, these things grew into love, loyalty, and friendships. On the other hand, if you plant seeds of doubt, evil, wrongdoing, these things grew up and manifested as bad relationships, conflicts, and trials and tribulations. I always wanted to sow good.

14. Be kind to everyone you meet, you never know what that person is going through.

This was the saying that has provided me the ability to work with individuals from all walks of life. It actually helped shape my personality. My Mother was preparing me to be a Social Worker.

Mama also had some funny and unique sayings that I am sure was passed down to her. Below are a few of my favorites:

1. Girl, now you are cooking with natural gas.

When Mama said this one, I had to once again remember the context. If someone had accomplished a great feat, for example a promotion or getting a prestigious position. This is when she would use this one. Later, I figured it out. When my Mother was growing up, they cooked on wood burning stoves. The stories I heard, it was no easy feat, you had to chop the wood, haul it into the house, and start a fire. Boy, sounds tedious to me. Imagine going from wood burning to a gas stove?

2. Now that don't make Cat or Dog Sense.

Another favorite, I use all the time. When someone said or did something outrageous, this is when she would use this one.

3. There goes Aunt Hagar's Children.

Now this one, Mama used when someone in the community did something shameful. I have no clue who Aunt Hagar was. All I knew was that her children were known for cutting up and acting a fool. I was in my sixties reading the Bible, when I figured out where Mama got that saying from. Aunt Hagar was actually Sarah's servant who she asked to sleep with her husband. Most of us know how this story goes. Yes, Mama had a sense of humor

4. You gonna be left holding the bag.

This one was about the sum total of my sex education class with my Mother. When she talked about getting pregnant out of wedlock, she made it plain you will be stuck with raising the child alone. Whenever I heard, "stuck holding the bag" I wanted no part of what was in it be it good or bad!

5. Just Keep Right On Living.

This of all of her sayings, is the one that she used to shut you down when you thought you had all the answers. This is the point in your life when you feel "grown enough" to challenge her philosophy. Some call it *old fashion* in the new age. You really have to dig deep on this one. I use it all the time. Simply put, if you live long enough, you will at some point experience the same things your parents went through. To throw in another one, Mama said, **Ain't nothing new under the sun**. This in my opinion sums up the Cycle of Life. It might be a new age, a new day, however, history will repeat itself. I am now sixty-nine years old, and lived long enough to attest to the fact, Mama was right. I have lived long enough to see the things she told me manifest and become true.

When I re-read most of my Mother's sayings, I discovered most were built on biblical principles. This is the legacy she passed on to me which means more than gold. My Mother read the Bible, daily until she became so sick that she no longer felt that it was of any importance. I now incorporate her wisdoms in all that I do and all that I am and all that I will become.

Mama, had many more sayings that have sustained me through the years. This is *Mother's Wit* and it will save your life, save you from disappointments, and steer your life in the right direction. I encourage you to write down some of your Mother's favorite sayings, especially the ones that didn't seem to make sense as a child, but now that you are grown, you find yourself saying them to your kids and grandchildren.

Mama, I thank you for your Wisdom, it has served me well.

PROLOGUE

TRANSITIONS

Dear Mama, I have written this Chapter over and over again in my mind. The day you and I parted for the very last time. Prior to that last time. Unfortunately, I witnessed life leave your body years before your actual transition. The date and time is ingrained in my heart and in my spirit. It has taken me years to talk about it without bursting in tears. It started out as a happy time. Levonnia and I visited you in the Nursing Home, I will never forget how beautiful you looked. Someone had braided your beautiful hair and you were sitting in your wheel chair surrounded by other residents. When you saw us approaching, all I could see was your big smile and the light in your beautiful large brown eyes. You told everyone who we were and that we had flown all the way from California to Chicago to see you. It was one of the last pleasant memories of you. The plan was to get permission for a home visit which was granted. We wanted to spend some quality time with you.

You shared that you like the nursing home because they kept you clean and well cared for. I was pleased to hear that news, as I was so worried about you being in the same nursing home that your Father had passed away in. The plan was great, however, it had to be approved by your husband, Willie Johnson. (Family, please be aware that although you may be sibling or children of a loved one, if that person is married, he or she has control unless specially spelled out in your Medical Directive. I suggest if you don't have one, please make it a priority.)

Well, permission for the home visit was granted, however, my Father denied it. He said that my Mother, his wife, could never return home again. When I questioned him, he simply said, if she comes home she will not want to return. I tried to convince him that she was happy where she was and only wanted to come home while we were in town. I told him she promised me that she would come back, a day before we left. He simply refused. I was given the difficult task to tell you that we could not bring you home, because her husband would not authorize it. Mama, when I told you the news, you simply said, "he is crazy." That day, I saw the light go out of your eyes. I knew that you would not live very long after this final disappointment and betrayal.

I returned to California, devastated with a broken heart. I, to this day, don't know how I manage to continue school and care for my family. It has taken years for me to forgive him. I eventually did. It has taken writing this legacy to you to heal my broken heart. Mama, I am at peace now.

Several months passed, after the above incident, however, you stopped talking. The doctors could find no medical reasons as to why you appeared to lose your ability to speak. In my heart, I believe that you simply were shutting down and retreating inside where you felt safe and protected. I continued to fly in for visits as often as possible. It was always a comfort to see you looking serene and peaceful.

The last visit was in July 1994, I started Graduate school in August 1993. I flew in because I received the news that you were in the hospital. When I arrived in Chicago, I drove directly to the hospital. We hugged and I was so happy to see you. You did not appear to be in any pain.

During that visit, I gave you permission to leave this world and return to the spiritual world.

I spent the entire visit, telling you that you should be so proud of the woman you have raised. I told you that you always worried about Frederick and Levonnia and that they were grown. You prayed to live long enough to see them grow up. I told you all the wonderful things that every child should tell their parents. How much I loved you, what a wonderful grandmother you had been to my children, and most of all I gave you permission to make your transition.

I thanked you for everything you did for me. I wanted you to know that we would be alright. During the visit, you began to sweat profusely. I remember taking a towel and wiping your face. I can only compare this experience with how Jesus must have felt when he was washing the feet of his disciples. In his case, he knew he was dying, however he loved them so much he wanted to serve them one last time. Mama, this is how I felt, I was honored to serve you one last time, it was such a feeling of love to touch you, to lovingly wipe the sweat from your brow, and it reminded me of how many times when I was a young child you did the same thing for me. Soon after, when I saw that you were resting, I said my goodbye.

PROLOGUE

My Mother, Ola M. Sutton Johnson born February 28, 1922 made her transition on September 14, 1994, two months after our last visit. I was not surprised to receive the call that she had passed away. No one asked me if I was alone, they just matter factly shared the news. My faith sustained me. We had already said our goodbyes. To the surprise of many, I did not return to Chicago for the funeral. Funerals are for the living, not for the person who is being celebrated. My philosophy is to give flowers while you are able to smell and appreciate them.

To say that I did not experience profound grief is an understatement. I decided to drop out of Graduate school. I felt no need to finish. You see, I wanted to save you. It all seems fruitless. However, the God in Heaven, sent two dear friends to call me. In doing so, they asked why I was not in school. Mama, I know that was your spirit. I got dressed and drove to USC. Even though I showed up late, my professor, Dr. Ferell Mennon, showed me grace and yet admonished me for being late. She understood my grief, however warned me I had a paper due. The rest is history.

In closing, I wish to convey to each of you to honor your parents, guardians, and caregivers while they are alive. Spend some time learning about their life, history, and favorite sayings. If you do so, it is a gift that will keep on giving.

BIBLIOGRAPHY

Christensen, Stephanie. "The Great Migration." blackpast.org. Accessed January 1, 2021. https://www.blackpast.org/african-american-history/great- migration-1915-1960/

ABOUT THE AUTHOR

Jurline K. Redeaux, MSW Director of New Impression Social Services Agency, holds a Masters in Social Work Degree from the University of Southern California. Upon retiring from Los Angeles County Department of Children and Family Services in 2008, as a Supervising Children's Social Worker, she founded New Impression, a 501(c) 3 nonprofit agency with two other social workers. New Impression advocates for the elimination of stigma associated with mental health, provides cancer supportive services, and aims to eliminate health care disparities.

She is a seasoned child welfare advocate with over 20 years of experience who has worked tirelessly throughout her career on the behalf of underrepresented populations, mainly women and children. She is so passionate about working with foster youth and their families, that in 2013, she came out of retirement to work part time for Los Angeles County DCFS to help reconnect foster youth with their families.

In 2017 she was diagnosed with endometrial cancer. She is into her second year of survivorship. In March 2019, she was selected by ECANA (Endometrial Cancer Action Network for African Americans) founded by Dr. Kemi Doll, to join their organization as a Community Empowerment Partner. She was trained at their first ECANA Conference in Hawaii and now is a certified Community Empowerment Partner. In this role, Jurline is educating and giving her personal testimony to the African American Community about facts associated with endometrial/uterine cancer.

UPCOMING TITLES

Ten Central Tenets of Social Work

Jurline is available for Training,
Conferences, and Consultations.
Please reach out to:
Jurline Redeaux
Website: www.jurlineredeaux.com
Email: jredeaux@newimpression.org

www.ingramcontent.com/pod-product-compliance
Lightning Source LLC
Chambersburg PA
CBHW021736180426
43194CB00059B/603